D1545563

All I can really
say. a friend
will always
remain.

Love
in
Jesus

The Poetry of Friendship

The Poetry
Of Friendship

A Collection of Favorite Verses

Selected by Beverly Simmons Bearly

Illustrated by Lana Slaton

HALLMARK EDITIONS

THE POETRY OF FRIENDSHIP

THE WORLD
IS FULL OF BEAUTY

The world is full of beauty—
Sparkling seas,
A garden in full bloom,
The shape of trees,
A child's eyes dancing
With some new delight,
A sky ablaze with stars
All twinkling bright,
A sun-splashed meadow's gold,
The rainbow's end . . .
But more than these—the love
Of friend for friend.

Katherine Nelson Davis

WHAT IS A FRIEND?

A friend is a person
   of great understanding
Who shares all our hopes
   and our schemes,
A companion who listens
   with infinite patience
To all of our plans and our dreams,
A true friend can make all our cares
   melt away
With the touch of a hand or a smile,
And with calm reassurance
   make everything brighter,
And life always seem more worth while—
A friend shares so many bright moments
   of laughter
At even the tiniest thing—
What memorable hours
   of light-hearted gladness
And pleasure this sharing can bring!
A friend is a cherished
   and precious possession
Who knows all our hopes and our fears,

And someone to treasure deep down
    in our hearts
With a closeness that grows
    through the years!

Cecil Nelson

THE COIN

Into my heart's treasury
    I slipped a coin
That time cannot take
    Nor a thief purloin—
Oh better than the minting
    Of a gold-crowned king
Is the safe-kept memory
    Of a lovely thing.

Sara Teasdale

THE KINDLY NEIGHBOR

I have a kindly neighbor, one who stands
Beside my gate and chats with me awhile.
Gives me the glory of his radiant smile
And comes at times to help
    with willing hands.
No station high or rank this man commands;
He, too, must trudge, as I,
    the long day's mile;
And yet, devoid of pomp or gaudy style,
He has a worth exceeding stocks or lands.

To him I go when sorrow's at my door;
On him I lean when burdens come my way;
Together oft we talk our trials o'er,
And there is warmth
    in each good night we say.
A kindly neighbor!
    Wars and strife shall end
When man has made
    the man next door his friend.

Edgar A. Guest

COMPLETENESS

My house is swept from roof to stone,
The windows sparkle in the light;
Silver and delph gleam on the board,
The polished wood and walls delight.
A table sits beside the hearth,
The bubbling kettle speaks of tea,
And best of all, a lovely friend
Has come to share an hour with me.

Katherine Edelman

THE MONK
AND THE PEASANT

A peasant once unthinkingly
   Spread tales about a friend.
But later found the rumors false
   And hoped to make amend.

He sought the counsel of a monk,
   A man esteemed and wise,
Who heard the peasant's story through
   And felt he must advise.

The kind monk said: "If you would have
   A mind again at peace,
I have a plan whereby you may
   From trouble find release.

"Go fill a bag with chicken down
   And to each dooryard go
And lay one fluffy feather where
   The streams of gossip flow."

The peasant did as he was told
   And to the monk returned,
Elated that his penance was
   A thing so quickly earned.

"Not yet," the old monk sternly said,
　"Take up your bag once more
And gather up the feathers that
　You placed at every door."

The peasant, eager to atone,
　Went hastening to obey,
No feathers met his sight, the wind
　Had blown them all away.

Margaret E. Bruner

TRUE TO THE BEST

Long years of pleasant friendship
　　may be broken
　By one hour's work
　　with thoughtless word or deed.
Yet why forget the thousand good words
　　spoken,
　The kindly help which met
　　a passing need?

We do not spurn the sunlight
　　when 'tis hidden;
　We look for good
　　when fiercest storms descend.
Then why lose faith, when undeserved,
　　unbidden,
　We meet disloyal usage from a friend?

Benjamin Keech

LITTLE THINGS

It's just the little homely things,
    The unobtrusive, friendly things,
The "won't-you-let-me-help-you" things
    That make our pathway light—
And it's just the jolly, joking things,
    The "never-mind-the-trouble" things
The "laugh-with-me, it's funny" things
    That make the world seem bright.

For all the countless famous things,
    The wondrous, record-breaking things,
Those "never-can-be-equalled" things
    That all the papers cite,
Aren't like the little human things,
    The everyday-encountered things,
The "just-because-I-like-you" things
    That make us happy quite.

So here's to all the simple things,
    The dear "all-in-a-day's-work" things,
The "smile-and-face-your-troubles" things,
    Trust God to put them right!

The "done-and-then-forgotten" things,
    The "can't-you-see-I-love-you" things,
The hearty "I-am-with-you" things
    That make life worth the fight.

Author Unknown

A FRIEND

There is no friend like an old friend
Who has shared our morning days,
No greeting like his welcome,
    No homage like his praise.
Fame is the scentless sunflower,
    With gaudy crown of gold;
But friendship is the breathing rose,
    With sweets in every fold.

Oliver Wendell Holmes

FRIENDSHIP

Into the melodious symphony of life
    A magic chord
       is sometimes clearly heard,
Lending a deeper meaning to the strain,
    Translated to the heart
       without a word.

Across the years forever it vibrates:
    Time cannot still the memory
       of its power;
Distance does not its beauty e'er efface,
    For in the heart it dwells—
       a lovely flower.

This golden chord
    of love and friendship sounds
    The theme, that is the music's melody;
It softens all the harsher notes of life,
    And makes the whole a happy harmony.

Dorothy Sproule

ON FRIENDSHIP

And a youth said, Speak to us of Friendship.
And the prophet answered, saying:
Your friend is your needs answered.
He is your field which you sow with love
    and reap with thanksgiving.
And he is your board and your fireside.
For you come to him with your hunger,
    and you seek him for peace . . .

When you part from a friend, you grieve not;
For that which you love most in him
    may be clearer in his absence,
    as the mountain to the climber
    is clearer from the plain.
And let there be no purpose in friendship
    save the deepening of the spirit.
For love that seeks aught but the disclosure
    of its own mystery is not love,
    but a net cast forth:
    and only the unprofitable is caught.

And let your best be for your friend.
If he must know the ebb of your tide,
    let him know its flood also.

For what is your friend that you should seek him
    with hours to kill?
Seek him always with hours to live.
For it is his to fill your need,
    but not your emptiness.
And in the sweetness of friendship
    let there be laughter,
    and sharing of pleasures.
For in the dew of simple things
    the heart finds its morning
    and is refreshed.

Kahlil Gibran

FRIENDSHIP

Oh, who will walk a mile with me,
    Along life's merry way?
A comrade blithe and full of glee,
Who dares to laugh out loud and free,
    And let his frolic fancy play,
    Like a happy child,
        through the flowers gay
    That fill the field and fringe the way,
Where he walks a mile with me.

And who will walk a mile with me,
    Along life's weary way?
A friend whose heart has eyes to see
The stars shine out
        o'er the darkening lea,
    And the quiet rest
      at the end of the day—
    A friend who knows, and dares to say,
    The brave, sweet words
      that cheer the way
Where he walks a mile with me.

With such a comrade, such a friend,
I fain would walk till journeys end,
　　Through summer sunshines, winter rain,
And then? Farewell, we shall meet again!
Henry van Dyke

THE HUMAN TOUCH

'Tis the human touch in this world
　　that counts,
　The touch of your hand and mine,
Which means far more
　　to the fainting heart
　Than shelter and bread and wine;
For shelter is gone
　　when the night is o'er,
　And bread lasts only a day,
But the touch of the hand,
　　the sound of the voice
　Sing on in the soul alway.
Spencer Michael Free

THE FRIEND
WHO JUST STANDS BY

When trouble comes your soul to try,
You love the friend who just "stands by."
Perhaps there's nothing he can do—
The thing is strictly up to you;
For there are troubles all your own,
And paths the soul must tread alone;
Times when love cannot smooth the road
Nor friendship lift the heavy load,
But just to know you have a friend
Who will "stand by" until the end,
Whose sympathy through all endures,
Whose warm handclasp is always yours—
It helps, someway, to pull you through,
Although there's nothing he can do.
And so with fervent heart you cry,
"God bless the friend who just 'stands by.'"

B. Y. Williams

A SHADY FRIEND
FOR TORRID DAYS

A shady friend for torrid days
Is easier to find
Than one of higher temperature
For frigid hour of mind.

The vane a little to the east
Scares muslin souls away;
If broadcloth breasts are firmer
Than those of organdy,

Who is to blame? The weaver?
Ah! the bewildering thread!
The tapestries of paradise
So notelessly are made!

Emily Dickinson

COMPARISONS

Friendship—Like music heard on the waters,
Like pines when the wind passeth by,
Like pearls in the depths of the ocean,
Like stars that enamel the sky,
Like June and the odor of roses,
Like dew and the freshness of morn,
Like sunshine that kisseth the clover,
Like tassels of silk on the corn,
Like mountains that arch the blue heavens,
Like clouds when the sun dippeth low,
Like songs of birds in the forest,
Like brooks where the sweet waters flow,
Like dreams of Arcadian pleasures,
Like colors that gratefully blend,
Like everything breathing of kindness—
Like these is the love of a friend.

A. P. Stanley

FRIENDSHIP IS
A SHELTERING TREE

Flowers are lovely; love is flower-like;
    Friendship is a sheltering tree;
Oh, the joys that came down shower-like,
    Of friendship, love and liberty,
        Ere I was old!

Samuel Taylor Coleridge

TO FRIENDSHIP

A friend is someone lovely, who
Cuts her chrysanthemums for you
And, giving, cares not for the cost,
Nor sees the blossoms she has lost;
But rather, values friendship's store
Gives you her best and grows some more.

Eleanor Long

THE CLASP
OF A FRIENDLY HAND

It isn't the gold that glitters,
   That fills your heart with cheer;
It isn't always the winning
   That brings you that happy tear.

We struggle to gain our objective,
   We hear the applause of the land—
But the thing that quickens the heart-beat
   Is the clasp of a friendly hand.

For a day the whole world's applauding,
   But we silently look for the friend
Who knows our true worth and stands by us
   Steadfastly until the end.

Stella Spencer

FRIENDS!

If all the sorrows of this weary earth—
   The pains and heartaches of humanity—
   If all were gathered up and given me,
I still would have my share
    of wealth and worth
   Who have you, Friend of Old,
    to be my cheer
   Through life's uncertain fortunes,
    year by year.

Thank God for friends, who dearer grow
    as years increase
   Who, as possessions fail our hopes
    and hands,
   Become the boon supreme,
    than gold and lands
More precious. Let all else,
    if must be, cease;
   But, Lord of Life, I pray on me bestow
   The gift of friends,
    to share the way I go.

Thomas Curtis Clark

DISCOVERY

Today a man discovered gold and fame;
Another flew the stormy seas;
Another saw an unnamed world aflame;
One found the germ of a disease;
But what high fates my paths attend:
For I—today I found a friend.

Helen Baker Parker

from LOYALTY

He may be six kinds of a liar,
    He may be ten kinds of a fool,
He may be a wicked highflyer
    Beyond any reason or rule;
There may be a shadow above him
    Of ruin and woes to impend,
And I may not respect, but I love him,
    Because—well, because he's my friend.

I criticize him but I do it
    In just a frank, comradely key,
And back-biting gossips will rue it
    If ever *they* knock him to me!
I never make diagrams of him,
    No maps of his soul have I penned;
I don't analyze—I just love him,
    Because—well, because he's my friend.

Berton Braley

TRUE FRIENDSHIP

True friendship, rare as precious gold,
And as enduring to the touch of time,
Exquisite as fine lace or filigree,
As mellow as the taste of vintage wine.

True friendship, subtle as old tapestry,
As undemanding as a candle flame,
Unchanging as an ageless work of art
That grows in worth as it remains the same.

Mary R. Hurley

TO A FRIEND

There is no room in your garden of love
For thorny patches
Dry with the drought of fear
Crowded by weeds of insincerity and doubt
For yours is a garden fair—
The garden of your heart
Blossoming with faith
Hedged in by truth
Truth blown by the winds of experience,
Wet by the showers
   of deep love and understanding.

I stand within your garden,
   filled with gratitude and awe,
Holding tenderly the blossoms
   and the roots
Which you have shared with me!

Iola Elliott Ueblacker

FRIENDSHIP

A sparkling, cheerful tongue
    will kindly greetings breed.
Of multitudes of friends sweet language
    is the seed.
Remain at peace with many, but
One counselor in a thousand heed.

Truly love your time-tried friend,
    guard his secrets well,
Lest he escape your snare
    as does a young gazelle.
No hope at all there is for him
Who itches madly till he tell.

Forsake no old-time friend
    you have found good and true.
Within one's life how many come
    one's heart to woo
With bitter drink that stings the tongue!
Far better is old wine than new.

In prosperous days how can a man tell
    who's his friend?
His enemies in secret hate,
    yet greetings send.

Halt! Fate puffs out an evil wind
Enemies laugh and friendships end.

Measure your friend.
    Perhaps he is a table friend
Who will for food and drink
    your maidens boldly send.
Ah, in one faithful, time-tried friend
Both medicine and treasure blend!

Be good to your friend. No miser be,
    although you save.
You soon will leave what gold
    to you good fortune gave.
You will not need your money then,
There are no dainties in the grave.

Better reprove your friend,
    if he has used you ill,
Than silent to remain
    and harbor anger still.
If he confess his fault, rejoice,
Cleave fast to him with all your will.

Max Ehrmann

SUNSHINE AND MUSIC

A laugh is just like sunshine.
It freshens all the day,
It tips the peak of life with light,
And drives the clouds away.
The soul grows glad that hears it
And feels its courage strong.
A laugh is just like sunshine
For cheering folks along.

A laugh is just like music.
It lingers in the heart,
And where its melody is heard
The ills of life depart;
And happy thoughts come crowding
Its joyful notes to greet:
A laugh is just like music
For making living sweet.

Author Unknown

FRIENDSHIP

Oh, the comfort—the inexpressible comfort
   of feeling safe with a person,
Having neither to weigh thoughts,
Nor measure words—but pouring them
All right out—just as they are—
Chaff and grain together—
Certain that a faithful hand will
Take and sift them—
Keep what is worth keeping—
And with the breath of kindness
Blow the rest away.

           Dinah Maria Mulock Craik

OLD FRIENDS

Old friends are best I do agree,
  But to this fact I hold;
That everything must first be new
  Before it can be old.
That old friend whom you love so much,
  Who's staunch and true and bold;
Was brand new on the day you met,
  Tho' now you call him old.
So make new friends each passing day
  The years quickly unfold;
And new friends whom you make today
  Will soon be classed as old.
And then you'll have a store of wealth
  That far surpasses gold;
For all the friends who now are new
  You'll soon be calling old.

Alice Cotterill

FRIENDSHIP

The richest yield of friendship
　　Is trustfulness complete,
Wherein is thought ne'er hidden
　　In prudent, far retreat,

But in the simple language
　　Of loyal brotherhood
It speaks in touch or glances
　　So certain understood.

Caroline Edwards Prentiss

FRIENDS WHO SAIL TOGETHER

There are friends who pass like ships
   in the night,
Who meet for a moment, then sail
   out of sight,
With never a backward glance of regret—
Friends we know briefly,
   then quickly forget . . .
There are other friends who sail together
Through quiet waters and stormy weather,
Helping each other through joy
   and through strife—
And they are the kind
   who give meaning to life!

Mary Dawson Hughes

FRIENDSHIP

Friendship needs no studied phrases,
    Polished face, or winning wiles;
Friendship deals no lavish praises,
    Friendship dons no surface smiles.

Friendship follows Nature's diction,
    Shuns the blandishments of Art,
Boldly severs truth from fiction,
    Speaks the language of the heart.

Friendship favors no condition,
    Scorns a narrow-minded creed,
Lovingly fulfills its mission,
    Be it word or be it deed.

Friendship cheers the faint and weary,
    Makes the timid spirit brave,
Warns the erring, lights the dreary,
    Smooths the passage to the grave.

Friendship–pure, unselfish friendship,
    All through life's allotted span,
Nurtures, strengthens, widens, lengthens,
    Man's relationship with man.

Author Unknown

from LIFE'S MIRROR

Give love, and love to your life
    will flow,
A strength in your utmost need,
Have faith, and a score of hearts
    will show
Their faith in your word and deed.

Give truth, and your gift will be paid
    in kind;
And honor will honor meet;
And a smile that is sweet
    will surely find
A smile that is just as sweet.

Madeline Bridges

FRIENDLY WORDS

A young rose in the summertime
Is beautiful to me,
And glorious the many stars
That glisten o'er the sea;
But friendly words at twilight hour
And hands to clasp my own,
Are sweeter than the fairest flowers
Or stars that ever shone.

The sun may warm the grass to life,
The dew the drooping flower,
And hearts grow bright that watch the light
Of summer's opening hour;
But words that breathe of tenderness
And hearts we know are true
Are warmer than the summertime
And brighter than the dew.

It is not much the world can give
With all its subtle art;
And gold and gems are not the things
To satisfy the heart.

William Sumner Hughes

SEEDS OF KINDNESS

If you have a friend worth loving,
    Love him. Yes, and let him know
That you love him, ere life's evening
    Tinge his brow with sunset glow.
Why should good words ne'er be said
Of a friend—till he is dead?

If you hear a song that thrills you,
    Sung by any child of song,
Praise it. Do not let the singer
    Wait deserved praises long.
Why should one who thrills your heart
Lack the joy you may impart?

If you hear a prayer that moves you
    By its humble, pleading tone,
Join it. Do not let the seeker
    Bow before his God alone.
Why should not your brother share
The strength of "two or three" in prayer?

If you see the hot tears falling
    From a brother's weeping eyes
Share them. And by kindly sharing
    Own your kinship in the skies.

Why should anyone be glad
When another's heart is sad?

If a silvery laugh goes rippling
    Through the sunshine on his face,
Share it. 'Tis the wise man's saying—
    For both grief and joy a place.
There's health and goodness in the mirth
In which an honest laugh has birth.

If your work is made more easy
    By a friendly, helping hand,
Say so. Speak out brave and truly
    Ere the darkness veil the land.
Should a fellow worker near
Falter for a word of cheer?

Scatter thus your seeds of kindness
    All enriching as you go—
Leave them. Trust the Harvest-giver;
    He will make each seed to grow.
So until the happy end,
Your life shall never lack a friend.

Author Unknown

TO MY FRIEND

I have never been rich before,
    But you have poured
Into my heart's high door
    A golden hoard.

My wealth is the vision shared,
    The sympathy,
The feast of the soul prepared
    By you for me.

I look for no greater prize
    Than your soft voice.
The steadiness of your eyes
    Is my heart's choice.

I have never been rich before,
    But I divine
Your step on my sunlit floor
    And wealth is mine!

Anne Campbell

"LAMPS"

My friends are little lamps to me,
   Their radiance warms
      and cheers my ways.
And all my pathway dark and lone
   Is brightened by their rays.
I try to keep them bright by faith,
   And never let them dim with doubt,
For every time I lose a friend
   A little lamp goes out.

Elizabeth Whittemore

CONFIDE IN A FRIEND

When you're tired and worn
    at the close of day
And things just don't seem
    to be going your way,
When even your patience
    has come to an end,
Try taking time out
    and confide in a friend.

Perhaps he too may have walked
    the same road
With a much troubled heart
    and burdensome load,
To find peace and comfort
    somewhere near the end,
When he stopped long enough
    to confide in a friend.

For then are most welcome
    a few words of cheer,
For someone who willingly
    lends you an ear.

No troubles exist
  that time cannot mend,
But to get quick relief,
  just confide in a friend.

Author Unknown

OLD FRIENDSHIPS
ARE THE DEAREST

Though many of life's pleasures
May change from year to year,
Old friendships never change at all
Except to grow more dear,
And just like cherished memories,
They have a place apart —
A place reserved forever
In a corner of the heart.

Barbara Burrow

JOY

Joy breathes in the sweet airs of spring,
   And in the shy wild blossom hides,
And soars upon the swallow's wing,
   And with the singing water glides.

Where lilies stand, a fragrant crowd,
   Rocked by the warm south wind he lies;
And dreams upon the balmy cloud
   Soft floating in the tender skies;

Shines clear from out the crescent sharp,
   Glittering above the sunset's red,
And of the west wind makes a harp,
   And gleams in starlight overhead.

Joy mantles in the golden wine,
   Joy to earth's humblest doth descend,
And looks at me with cheer divine
   From out the dear eyes of my friend.

Celia Thaxter

MY HOUSE OF FRIENDSHIP

I built a house of friendship
    through the years
Each block a kindly thought
    is held in place
By mortar made of tenderness and tears
For others woes. The rooms are large
    with space
For all my friends. There is no strain
    nor stress.
Foundation stones are love and loyalty,
And over all a roof of cheerfulness.
Mirrored upon the walls where we may see,
Are memories, some etched
    in brilliant hue
While some are dark;
    and down the corridors
Come echoes of glad voices old and new.
Times when my spirit droops
    or when it soars,
I find repose here where my travels end
The house that you have helped to build,
    my friend!

Alma Jeffries Stull

54

THE JOYS OF FRIENDSHIP

We just shake hands at meeting
With many that come nigh;
We nod the head in greeting
To many that go by,–
But welcome through the gateway
Our few old friends and true;
Then hearts leap up, and straightway
There's open house for you,
Old friends,
There's open house for you!

Gerald Massey

RUBIES

They brought me rubies from the mine,
   And held them to the sun;
I said, they are drops of frozen wine
   From Eden's vats that run.

I looked again,—I thought them hearts
   Of friends to friends unknown;
Tides that should warm each neighboring life
   Are locked in sparkling stone.

But fire to thaw that ruddy snow,
   To break enchanted ice,
And give love's scarlet tides to flow,—
   When shall that sun arise?

Ralph Waldo Emerson

WHAT IS A FRIEND?

What Is a Friend? I'll tell you.
It is a person with whom you dare
   to be yourself.
Your soul can go naked with him.
He seems to ask you to put on nothing,
   only to be what you really are,
When you are with him,
   you do not have to be on your guard.
You can say what you think,
   so long as it is genuinely you.
He understands those contradictions
   in your nature that cause others
   to misjudge you.
With him you breathe freely—
   you can avow your little vanities
   and envies and absurdities
   and in opening them up to him
   they are dissolved
   on the white ocean of his loyalty.
He understands.— You can weep with him,
   laugh with him, pray with him—
   through and underneath it all he sees,
   knows and loves you.
A Friend—I repeat—
   is *one with whom you dare to be yourself.*
                              Author Unknown

from UNDER THE WILLOWS

In June 't is good to lie beneath a tree
While the blithe season
   comforts every sense,
Steeps all the brain in rest,
   and heals the heart,
Brimming it o'er with sweetness unawares,
Fragrant and silent as that rosy snow
Wherewith the pitying apple-tree fills up
And tenderly lines
   some last-year robin's nest.
There muse I of old times,
   old hopes, old friends. . . .

James Russell Lowell

FRIENDSHIP HOUSE

The sun is always shining in . . . The home
where friendship lives . . . Where life is
measured not by tears . . . But by the joy
it gives . . . Where hands are clasped
in greeting and . . . The warmth of love
is shown . . . And every word is spoken in . . .
An understanding tone . . . The flowers
are forever fair . . . Where kindly thoughts
abide . . . Where there is never any room . . .
For jealousy or pride . . . Where sympathy
and sacrifice . . . And cheerfulness
prevail . . . And smiles of true
encouragement . . . Are like an endless
trail . . . The sun is always shining and . . .
The sky is always clear . . . Where
friendship lives and sentiments . . .
Are honest and sincere.

James J. Metcalfe

from DEDICATION

Not chance of birth or place
    has made us friends,
  Being oftentimes
    of different tongues and nations,
But the endeavor
    for the selfsame ends,
  With the same hopes,
    and fears, and aspirations.

Therefore I hope,
    as no unwelcome guest,
  At your warm fireside,
    when the lamps are lighted,
To have my place reserved
    among the rest,
  Nor stand as one
    unsought and uninvited!

Henry Wadsworth Longfellow

Set at The Castle Press
in Garamond, an old-face type
designed by Claude Garamond about 1530.
Printed on Hallmark Eggshell Book paper.
Designed by Lana Slaton.